# Chris Hadfield

by Chelsea Donaldson

Gail Saunders-Smith, PhD, Consulting Editor

CAPSTONE PRESS

a capstone imprint

Pebble Plus is published by Capstone Press,
1710 Roe Crest Drive, North Mankato, Minnesota 56003
www.capstonepub.com

Cataloging-in-publication information is on file with the Library of Congress.
Donaldson, Chelsea, 1959- author.
Chris Hadfield / by Chelsea Donaldson.
pages cm. — (Pebble plus. Canadian biographies)
Summary: "Simple text and full-color photographs describe the life of Chris Hadfield"— Provided by publisher.
Audience: Ages 4-8.
Audience: K to grade 3.
Includes bibliographical references and index.
ISBN 978-1-4914-1957-1 (library binding : alk. paper)
ISBN 978-1-4914-1976-2 (pbk. : alk. paper)
ISBN 978-1-4914-1989-2 (eBook PDF)
1.  Hadfield, Chris, 1959—Juvenile literature. 2.  Astronauts—Canada--Biography—Juvenile literature.
I. Title.
TL789.85.H34D66 2015
629.450092—dc23                                                 2014015715

**Developed and Produced by Focus Strategic Communications, Inc.**
Adrianna Edwards: project manager
Ron Edwards: editor
Rob Scanlan: designer and compositor
Karen Hunter: media researcher

**Photo Credits**
Chris Hadfield: 5 inset, 9, 11 (background, inset); Getty: AFP/Getty Images; NASA: cover, 5 (bckgrd), 7, 13, 15, 17, 21, title page.

## Note to Parents and Teachers
The Canadian Biographies set supports national curriculum standards for social studies related to people and culture. This book describes and illustrates Chris Hadfield. The images support early readers in understanding text. The repetition of words and phrases helps early readers learn new words. This book also introduces early readers to subject-specific vocabulary words, which are defined in the Glossary section. Early readers may need assistance to read some words and to use the Table of Contents, Glossary, Read More, Internet Sites, and Index sections of the book.

Printed in China by Leo Paper Group in 2014
007039LEOF14

# Table of Contents

Early Life. . . . . . . . . . . . . . . . . . . . . .4

Aiming High . . . . . . . . . . . . . . . . . .8

Life as an Astronaut . . . . . . . . . . . .12

Later Years . . . . . . . . . . . . . . . . .20


Glossary . . . . . . . . . . . . . . . . . . .22

Read More . . . . . . . . . . . . . . . . .23

Internet Sites. . . . . . . . . . . . . . . . .23

Index . . . . . . . . . . . . . . . . . . . . .24

# Early Life

Astronaut Chris Hadfield
was born August 29, 1959,
in Sarnia, Ontario. His father
was a pilot. Even as a child,
Chris loved planes.

born in Sarnia,
Ontario

1959

Chris at 5 years old in his own "spaceship"

Chris in a space shuttle in 1991

Chris grew up on a corn farm in Milton, Ontario. At age 9 he watched the first moon landing on TV. He knew then that he wanted to be an astronaut.

born in Sarnia, Ontario

1959

1969

watches first moon landing

6

U.S. astronauts first landed on the moon in 1969.

# Aiming High

After high school Chris joined the armed forces. He learned how to fly planes. He also studied mechanical engineering. In 1982 Chris graduated from Royal Military College.

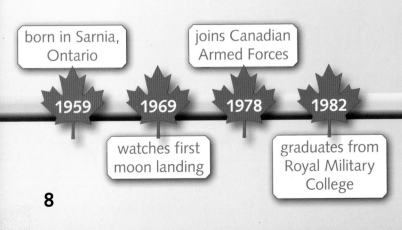

born in Sarnia, Ontario

joins Canadian Armed Forces

1959

1969

1978

1982

watches first moon landing

graduates from Royal Military College

Chris (far left) as a young cadet

In the late 1980s, Chris went
back to school. He learned
to be a test pilot. He flew
the fastest planes in the world.
He wanted to find ways
for pilots to fly safely.

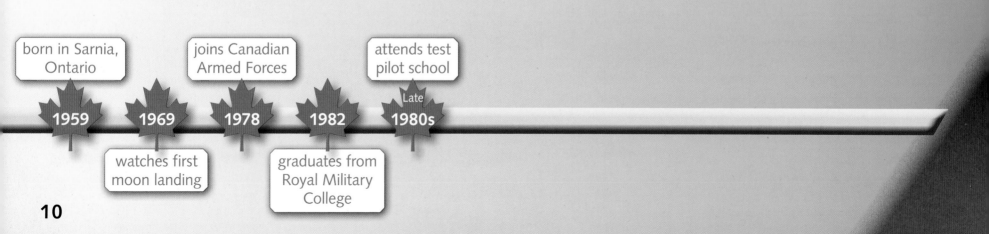

born in Sarnia,
Ontario

joins Canadian
Armed Forces

attends test
pilot school

Late

**1959**    **1969**    **1978**    **1982**    **1980s**

watches first
moon landing

graduates from
Royal Military
College

Chris as a test pilot

# Life as an Astronaut

In 1992 Chris made it into the Canadian Astronaut Program. Three years later Chris went on his first space flight. He stayed on the Mir Space Station for eight days.

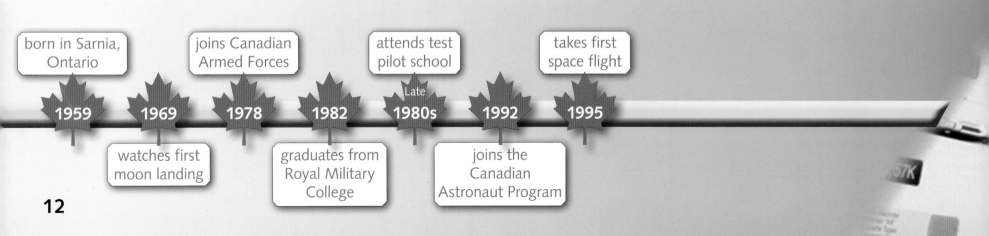

born in Sarnia, Ontario

joins Canadian Armed Forces

attends test pilot school

takes first space flight

Late

1959    1969    1978    1982    1980s    1992    1995

watches first moon landing

graduates from Royal Military College

joins the Canadian Astronaut Program

Chris playing his guitar on the MIR space station in 1995

In 2001 Chris blasted into space again. He brought a crane to the *International Space Station* (ISS). The crane was called the Canadarm. To place the crane, Chris had to do a space walk.

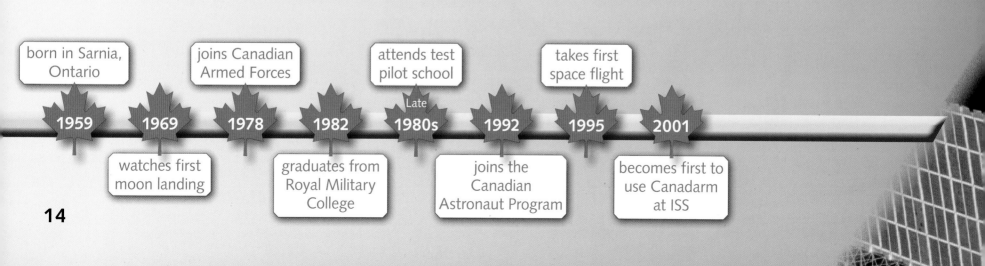

born in Sarnia, Ontario
1959

watches first moon landing
1969

joins Canadian Armed Forces
1978

graduates from Royal Military College
1982

attends test pilot school
Late 1980s

joins the Canadian Astronaut Program
1992

takes first space flight
1995

becomes first to use Canadarm at ISS
2001

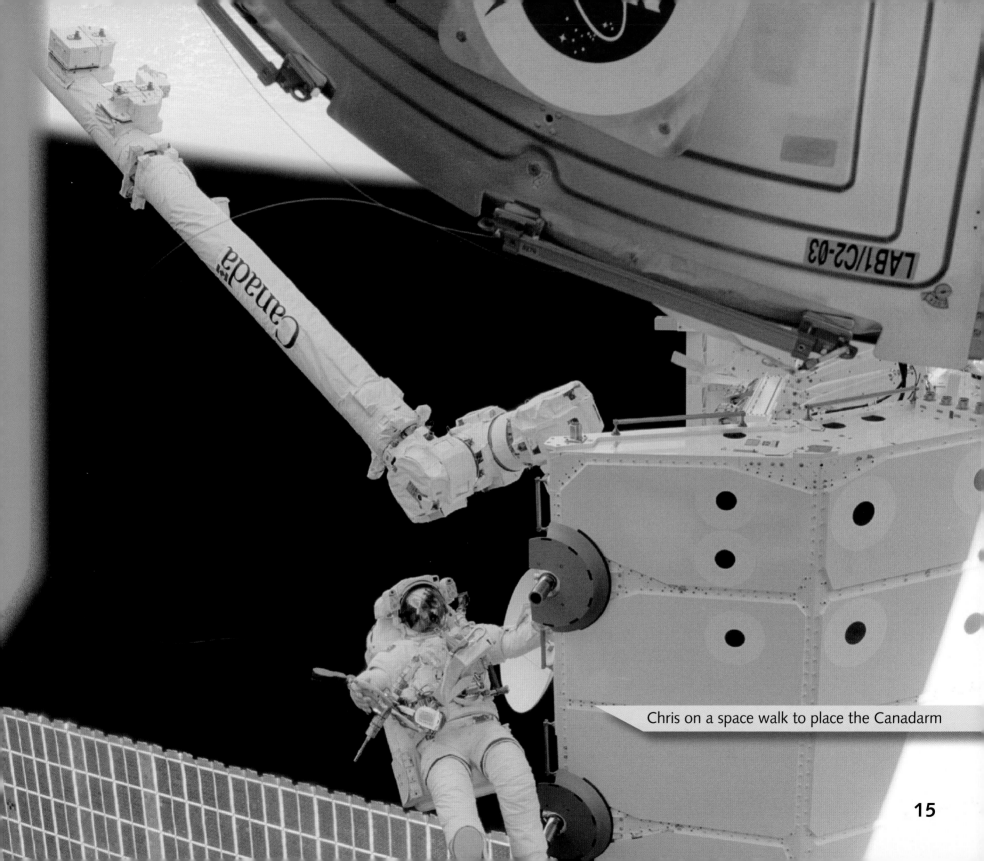

Chris on a space walk to place the Canadarm

Chris visited space for the last time in 2012. From the ISS he talked to students. He answered questions about life in space. He even recorded a song!

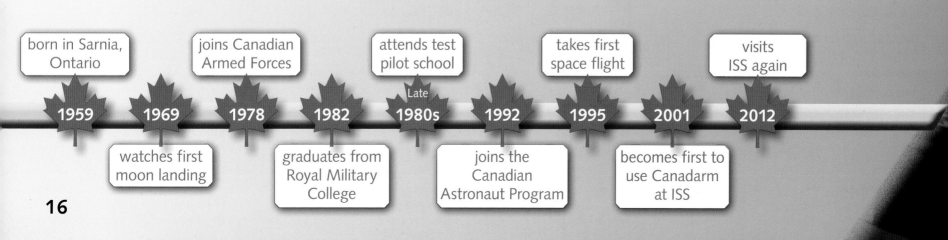

| born in Sarnia, Ontario | | joins Canadian Armed Forces | | attends test pilot school | | takes first space flight | | visits ISS again |
|---|---|---|---|---|---|---|---|---|
| **1959** | **1969** | **1978** | **1982** | Late **1980s** | **1992** | **1995** | **2001** | **2012** |
| | watches first moon landing | | graduates from Royal Military College | | joins the Canadian Astronaut Program | | becomes first to use Canadarm at ISS | |

Chris in space for the last time

Chris lived on the ISS for five months. He was the first Canadian commander of the ISS. Canadians were very proud!

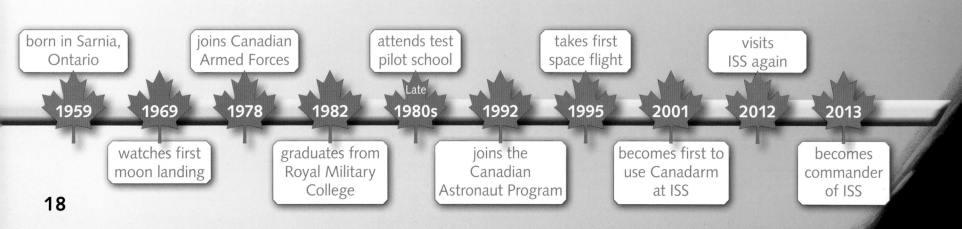

| born in Sarnia, Ontario | | joins Canadian Armed Forces | | attends test pilot school | | takes first space flight | | visits ISS again | |
|---|---|---|---|---|---|---|---|---|---|
| **1959** | **1969** | **1978** | **1982** | Late **1980s** | **1992** | **1995** | **2001** | **2012** | **2013** |
| | watches first moon landing | | graduates from Royal Military College | | joins the Canadian Astronaut Program | | becomes first to use Canadarm at ISS | | becomes commander of ISS |

Chris as ISS Commander

# Later Years

Chris returned to Earth in May 2013. Then he retired from the space program. He had lived his dream. He had also paved the way for many young people.

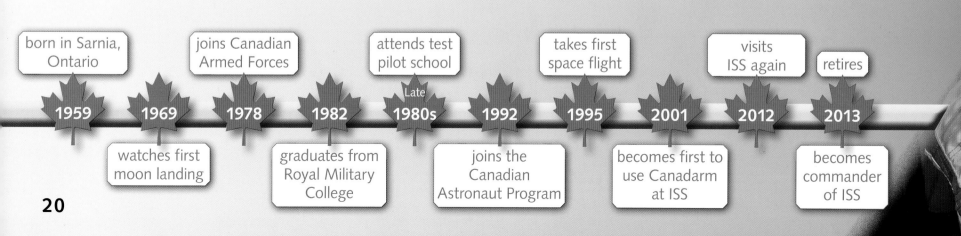

| born in Sarnia, Ontario | joins Canadian Armed Forces | attends test pilot school | takes first space flight | visits ISS again | retires |
|---|---|---|---|---|---|
| **1959** | **1969** | **1978** | **1982** | Late **1980s** | **1992** | **1995** | **2001** | **2012** | **2013** |
| | watches first moon landing | graduates from Royal Military College | joins the Canadian Astronaut Program | becomes first to use Canadarm at ISS | becomes commander of ISS |

Chris explains how an astronaut suit works.

# Glossary

**astronaut**—a person who is trained to live and work in space

**Canadarm**—a special crane for building and fixing the space station; the Canadarm was built by Canadian scientists

**commander**—a person in charge of the ISS

**International Space Station (ISS)**—a place for astronauts to live and work in space

**mechanical engineer**—a person who understands how engines and other machines work

**retire**—to give up work, usually because of a person's age

**space walk**—a period of time during which an astronaut leaves the spacecraft to move around in space

**test pilot**—a person who tests new airplanes

# Read More

**Down, Heather**. *Postcards from Space*. The Chris Hadfield Story. Barrie, ON: Wintertickle Press, 2013.

**Hughes, Catherine A**. *National Geographic Little Kids First Big Book of Space*. Des Moines, IA: National Geographic Children's Books, 2012.

# Internet Sites

FactHound offers a safe, fun way to find Internet sites related to this book. All of the sites on FactHound have been researched by our staff.

Here's all you do:

Visit *www.facthound.com*

Type in this code: 9781491419571

Check out projects, games and lots more at
www.capstonekids.com

# Index

astronaut, 4, 6, 12

birth, 4

Canadarm, 14

Canadian armed forces, 8

commander of ISS, 18

*International Space Station* (ISS),
    14, 16, 18

mechanical engineering, 8

Milton, ON, 6

Mir Space Station, 12

moon landing, 6

Ontario, 4, 6

pilot, 4, 8, 10

planes, 4, 8, 10

retiring, 20

Royal Military College, 8

Sarnia, ON, 4

school, 8, 10

space station, 12, 14

space walk, 14

test pilot, 10